CW01475933

Starting & Growing a Successful Tea Business

"A comprehensive Course"

By : Vineeta Prasad

Copyright © 2023 [Vineeta Prasad]. All rights reserved.

No part of this publication may be reproduced, stored in a retrieval system, or transmitted, in any form or by any means, electronic, mechanical, photocopying, recording, or otherwise, without the prior permission of the copyright owner.

This book is a work of fiction. Names, characters, places, and incidents either are the product of the author's imagination or are used fictitiously. Any resemblance to actual persons, living or dead, events, or locales is entirely coincidental.

This book is licensed for your personal enjoyment only. This book may not be re-sold or given away to other people. If you would like to share this book with another person, please purchase an additional copy for each recipient. If you're reading this book and did not purchase it, or it was not purchased for your use only, then please return to your favorite book retailer and purchase your own copy. Thank you for respecting the hard work of this author.

This course is designed to equip aspiring entrepreneurs with the knowledge and skills needed to start and grow a successful tea business.

Table of Contents

Introduction to the Tea Business
Chapter 1

Welcome to the "Starting and Growing a Successful Tea Business" course! In this first module, we will introduce you to the world of tea and the tea industry. We will explore the global tea market, the different types of tea, and the processes involved in tea production and processing.

Tea is the most popular beverage in the world, with over 2.5 million cups consumed every second. The tea industry is a multi-billion-dollar industry, and it is growing rapidly due to increasing demand for healthier beverage options. The tea market is diverse, with a range of products catering to different consumer preferences, including black tea, green tea, herbal tea, and flavored tea.

During this module, we will also discuss the properties and classifications of tea, including the differences between tea grades, types of tea, and the various tea-growing regions. You will learn how tea is grown, harvested, and processed to produce the final product. This knowledge will be valuable in sourcing high-quality tea leaves for your business.

By the end of this module, you will have a solid understanding of the tea industry, the different types of tea, and the processes involved in tea production and processing. This knowledge will serve as a foundation for the rest of the course as we delve deeper into the tea business, including sourcing and blending, tea brewing and tasting, marketing and sales, and managing a tea business.

Introduction to the global tea market

The global tea market is a vast industry that encompasses production, processing, distribution, and consumption of tea. Tea is the second most consumed beverage in the world after water. The global tea market is growing at a steady pace, driven by the increasing demand for healthier and natural beverages. According to a report by Grand View Research, the global tea market size was valued at $52.8 billion in 2019 and is projected to reach $81.6 billion by 2027, with a CAGR of 5.5% from 2020 to 2027.

Tea is produced in many countries worldwide, with China, India, and Kenya being the largest producers and exporters of tea. Other tea-producing countries include Sri Lanka, Japan, Turkey, Vietnam, Indonesia, and Bangladesh. The tea industry provides employment to millions of people worldwide, from tea farmers to factory workers, tea tasters, and traders.

The tea market is diverse, with a range of products catering to different consumer preferences. Black tea is the most consumed type of tea, followed by green tea, herbal tea, and flavored tea. The demand for specialty teas, such as organic, fair trade, and single-estate teas, is also increasing.

The tea market is segmented by packaging type, distribution channel, and application. Tea is available in loose-leaf, tea bags, and ready-to-drink formats. The distribution channels include supermarkets and hypermarkets, convenience stores, online retailers, and tea shops. Tea is used for different applications, including hot tea, iced tea, and functional tea.

Understanding the global tea market is crucial for any tea business owner. Knowing the market trends, consumer preferences, and the competition will help you make informed decisions about your tea business. In the next modules, we will delve deeper into the tea business, including tea sourcing and blending, tea brewing and tasting, marketing and sales, and managing a tea business.

Types of tea and their properties

Tea comes in many types and varieties, each with its unique flavor, aroma, and health benefits. The main types of tea are:

1. **Black Tea:** Black tea is the most common and widely consumed type of tea globally. It is made from fully oxidized tea leaves, resulting in a robust, bold flavor and a deep reddish-brown color. Black tea contains caffeine and has antioxidants that can help reduce the risk of heart disease and stroke.

2. **Green Tea:** Green tea is made from unoxidized tea leaves, giving it a lighter flavor and a pale green color. It is rich in antioxidants called catechins, which have been shown to have various health benefits, such as reducing the risk of cancer and cardiovascular disease.

3. **White Tea**: White tea is made from young tea leaves and buds that are picked before they are fully open. It has a delicate, light flavor and a pale yellow color. White tea is the least processed of all tea types and contains high levels of antioxidants and low caffeine.

4. **Oolong Tea**: Oolong tea is a partially oxidized tea that falls between green tea and black tea in terms of oxidation level. It has a complex flavor profile that can range from floral and fruity to nutty and woody, depending on the degree of oxidation. Oolong tea has a moderate amount of caffeine and antioxidants.

5. **Herbal Tea:** Herbal tea is not technically tea, as it is not made from the tea plant Camellia sinensis. Instead, it is made from a variety of herbs, flowers, fruits, and spices. Herbal tea is caffeine-free and has various health benefits, depending on the ingredients used.

Understanding the properties of each tea type is crucial for a tea business owner. Knowing the flavor profile, aroma, and health benefits of each tea type will help you source and blend teas that cater to your customers' preferences. In the next modules, we will discuss tea sourcing and blending techniques that will help you create unique and delicious tea blends.

Understanding tea grades and classifications

Tea grading and classification systems are used to differentiate teas based on their quality, flavor, and appearance. Here are some common tea grading and classification systems:

1. **Black Tea:** In the orthodox tea production method, black teas are graded based on leaf size and quality. The grading scale ranges from whole leaf teas to broken leaf teas, fannings, and dust. Whole leaf teas are considered the highest quality, while fannings and dust are used for tea bags and blends.

2. **Green Tea:** Green teas are generally not graded, but some Japanese green teas are classified based on leaf quality and processing methods. For example, the highest grade of Japanese green tea is called Gyokuro, which is made from shade-grown tea leaves.

3. **White Tea:** White teas are also not graded, but the highest quality white teas are made from young tea buds and leaves, hand-picked in early spring.

4. **Oolong Tea:** Oolong teas are graded based on leaf size, shape, and oxidation level. The grading scale ranges from tightly rolled balls to large, open leaves. Higher grade oolong teas are generally more complex in flavor and aroma.

5. **Pu-erh Tea:** Pu-erh teas are aged and fermented, and they are classified based on the year of production, region, and quality. The highest quality pu-erh teas are aged for many years and have a complex, earthy flavor and aroma.

Understanding tea grading and classification systems will help tea business owners source and purchase high-quality teas that meet their customers' expectations. It is important to note that different regions and countries may use different grading and classification systems, so it is essential to research and understand the specific systems used for the teas you plan to sell.

Overview of tea production and processing

Tea production and processing can vary depending on the type of tea being produced, but here is a general overview of the process:

1. **Plucking:** Tea leaves are hand-picked or machine-harvested depending on the region and type of tea.

2. **Withering:** The tea leaves are spread out in a cool, dry area to wilt and lose some of their moisture. This process makes the leaves pliable and reduces the bitter taste.

3. **Rolling:** The leaves are rolled to break down the cell walls and release the tea juices, which helps to develop the tea's flavor and aroma.

4. **Oxidation:** This step is only used in the production of black and oolong teas. The tea leaves are spread out in a humid environment to encourage oxidation, which turns the leaves brown and develops the flavor.

5. **Firing:** The leaves are dried to stop the oxidation process and preserve the tea's flavor and aroma.

6. **Sorting and Grading:** The tea leaves are sorted by size and quality using different grading systems, depending on the region and type of tea.

7. **Packaging:** The tea is packaged into bags or loose-leaf containers and sent to wholesalers or retailers.

Understanding the tea production and processing steps will help tea business owners select and purchase high-quality teas that meet their customers' expectations. It is also essential to consider the environmental and social impact of tea production and processing, and to source teas from ethical and sustainable producers.

Tea Sourcing and Blending
Chapter 2

Tea sourcing and blending are critical components of a successful tea business. Here is an overview of each:

Tea Sourcing: Sourcing high-quality tea leaves is essential for creating delicious and unique tea blends that customers will love. Tea leaves can come from many regions around the world, and each region has its unique tea varieties and flavor profiles. When sourcing tea leaves, it is important to consider the following factors:

1. **Flavor:** Different regions produce tea leaves with different flavor profiles. For example, Chinese tea leaves are known for their floral and earthy flavors, while Indian tea leaves are known for their bold and robust flavors.

2. **Quality:** The quality of tea leaves can vary significantly depending on the region, season, and growing conditions. High-quality tea leaves will have a uniform shape, consistent color, and a fresh aroma.

3. **Sustainability:** Tea farming can have a significant impact on the environment, so it is essential to source tea from sustainable and ethical producers who use responsible farming practices.

Tea Blending: Blending different types of tea leaves can create unique and delicious tea blends. When blending tea leaves, it is important to consider the following factors:

1. **Flavor profile:** Each type of tea has its unique flavor profile, so it's important to balance the flavors when blending. For example, black teas are bold and robust, while green teas are delicate and floral.
2. **Texture:** The texture of tea leaves can vary significantly, from fine and powdery to large and chunky. Blending tea leaves with different textures can create a more complex and interesting tea blend.

3. **Aroma:** The aroma of tea is a crucial component of its flavor. Blending tea leaves with complementary aromas can create a more complex and enjoyable tea experience.

Creativity: Blending tea is an art, and creativity is essential for creating unique and delicious tea blends. Experimenting with different tea varieties, flavor combinations, and brewing methods can lead to exciting new blends that customers will love.

In summary, tea sourcing and blending are critical components of a successful tea business. Sourcing high-quality tea leaves from sustainable and ethical producers, and blending them creatively, can create unique and delicious tea blends that customers will love.

Sourcing High-Quality Tea Leaves

Sourcing high-quality tea leaves is a crucial part of creating delicious and unique tea blends. Here are some tips for sourcing high-quality tea leaves:

1. **Know your suppliers: When sourcing tea leaves, it's essential to work with reputable suppliers who source their tea from high-quality producers. Do your research and look for suppliers who have a good reputation in the industry.**

Knowing your suppliers is crucial when sourcing tea leaves for your business. Here are some reasons why it's essential to work with reputable suppliers who source their tea from high-quality producers:

1. **Consistent quality:** Reputable suppliers who work with high-quality producers will be able to provide you with tea leaves that are consistently of high quality. This is essential for creating delicious tea blends and maintaining the loyalty of your customers.

2. **Transparency:** Working with reputable suppliers means that you can be confident that the tea leaves you are sourcing are ethically produced and sourced. This is important for creating a socially responsible and sustainable tea business.

3. **Reliability:** Reputable suppliers are reliable and can ensure that you receive your tea leaves on time and in the quantity you require. This is essential for maintaining a steady supply chain and ensuring that your business runs smoothly.

4. **Expertise:** Reputable suppliers have expertise in the tea industry and can provide you with valuable advice and guidance on tea sourcing, blending,

and other aspects of your business. This can help you make informed decisions and improve the quality of your tea blends.

Overall, working with reputable suppliers is essential for creating a successful tea business that produces high-quality and delicious tea blends. By doing your research and selecting the right suppliers, you can ensure that your business is built on a solid foundation of quality and transparency.

2. **Look for tea grown in the right conditions: The growing conditions for tea can impact its flavor and quality. Look for tea that is grown in ideal conditions, including the right altitude, soil, and climate.**

When sourcing tea leaves for blending, it's important to look for tea grown in the right conditions. Here are some reasons why:

1. **Flavor:** Tea that is grown in ideal conditions will have a better flavor profile, which is essential for creating high-quality and delicious tea blends. The altitude, soil, and climate in which tea is grown can all impact its flavor.

2. **Quality:** Tea that is grown in ideal conditions will have a better quality and higher nutritional value. This is important for creating a healthy and nutritious tea blend.

3. **Sustainability:** Tea that is grown in ideal conditions is more likely to be grown sustainably, with minimal impact on the environment. This is important for creating a socially responsible and environmentally friendly tea business.

4. **Reputation:** Tea that is grown in ideal conditions is often associated with a good reputation in the industry, which can help to build the reputation of your own tea business.

Overall, looking for tea grown in the right conditions is important for creating high-quality and sustainable tea blends. By paying attention to the growing conditions of the tea you source, you can ensure that your tea business is built on a foundation of quality and sustainability.

3. **Consider the season: The season in which the tea is harvested can impact its quality. The first flush of tea leaves is typically the highest quality, as they are the youngest and most tender leaves.**

When sourcing tea leaves for blending, it's important to consider the season in which the tea is harvested. Here's why:

1. **Quality:** The season in which the tea is harvested can impact its quality. The first flush of tea leaves, which is typically harvested in the spring, is considered the highest quality. These leaves are the youngest and most tender, and they have a delicate flavor profile. Later flushes, which are harvested in the summer and fall, have a stronger flavor and are considered lower quality.

2. **Availability:** The availability of tea can vary depending on the season. Some teas are only available during certain times of the year, so it's important to plan ahead and source your tea accordingly.

3. **Cost:** The cost of tea can also vary depending on the season. First flush teas, which are considered the highest quality, are often more expensive than later flushes. By considering the season in which the tea is harvested, you can plan your budget accordingly and ensure that you are getting the best value for your money.

Overall, considering the season in which the tea is harvested is important for ensuring that you are sourcing high-quality tea leaves that meet your needs as a tea blender. By paying attention to the season, you can plan your sourcing strategy, manage your budget, and create delicious and high-quality tea blends.

4. **Evaluate the tea's appearance:** High-quality tea leaves should be uniform in shape and size, with a consistent color and texture. Avoid tea leaves that have an uneven appearance, as this may indicate poor quality.

When sourcing tea leaves for blending, it's important to evaluate the tea's appearance to ensure that you are selecting high-quality leaves. Here's why:

1. **Appearance can indicate quality**: The appearance of the tea leaves can give you clues about their quality. High-quality tea leaves should be uniform in shape and size, with a consistent color and texture. This indicates that the leaves were harvested and processed properly.

2. **Avoid poor quality leaves:** Tea leaves that have an uneven appearance may indicate poor quality. For example, leaves that are broken or damaged may have a bitter taste or lack flavor. Leaves that are discolored or have an inconsistent texture may also be lower quality.

3. **Consistency is key:** When blending tea, it's important to use consistent tea leaves to ensure that your blends have a consistent flavor profile. By selecting tea leaves that have a uniform appearance, you can help ensure that your blends are consistent.

Overall, evaluating the appearance of tea leaves is an important part of sourcing high-quality leaves for blending. By selecting leaves that have a consistent appearance, you can help ensure that your blends are high-quality and have a consistent flavor profile.

5. **Smell the tea: High-quality tea leaves will have a fresh and fragrant aroma. Avoid tea leaves that have a musty or stale smell, as this may indicate poor quality.**

The aroma of the tea can give you an indication of its quality. The fragrance should be fresh and distinct, indicating that the tea leaves are of high quality. On the other hand, a musty or stale aroma may indicate that the tea leaves have been improperly stored or are of low quality. When evaluating the aroma, take note of any underlying scents or notes that are present. These can provide clues about the tea's flavor profile and potential for blending. It's important to remember that the aroma of the tea can be affected by the brewing process, so it's essential to take note of the fragrance of the dry leaves before brewing.

6. **Taste the tea: Taste is the ultimate test of tea quality. When sourcing tea leaves, it's essential to taste them to evaluate their flavor profile and quality.**

Tasting the tea is the most critical step in evaluating its quality. The flavor should be rich, complex, and well-balanced, with no off-flavors or bitterness. Take note of any underlying flavor notes, such as floral, fruity, or nutty flavors, as these can provide clues about the tea's origin and potential for blending. When tasting the tea, use freshly boiled water and follow the recommended brewing time and temperature for the particular tea. This will help to ensure that you are tasting the tea at its best. It's also important to taste the tea without any additives, such as milk or sugar, as these can mask the tea's natural flavors. Tasting tea can be a subjective experience, so it's a good idea to get feedback from others to ensure that you are evaluating the tea objectively. By tasting the tea, you can determine if it is of the quality you require and if it will be suitable for your intended blends or products.

By following these tips, you can source high-quality tea leaves that will form the foundation of your delicious and unique tea blends.

Factors to consider when selecting teas for blending

When selecting teas for blending, there are several factors to consider to ensure that the resulting blend is balanced and delicious. Here are some important factors to consider:

1. **Flavor profile:** The most important factor to consider when selecting teas for blending is their flavor profile. Each tea has its unique flavor profile, which can be influenced by factors such as origin, processing, and season. When selecting teas for blending, consider how their flavors will complement or contrast with each other.

To create a delicious and balanced tea blend, it's important to choose teas with complementary flavor profiles. For example, if you're blending a tea with a strong, bold flavor, you may want to balance it out with a milder, sweeter tea. Similarly, if you're blending a tea with a floral or fruity flavor, you may want to pair it with a more robust tea to add depth and complexity.

2. **Aroma:** A tea's aroma can greatly impact its overall flavor profile. When selecting teas for blending, pay attention to their aroma and consider how it will contribute to the final blend.

A tea's aroma is an important aspect to consider when selecting teas for blending because it can greatly impact the overall flavor profile. The aroma of a tea is influenced by its origin, processing, and storage. For example, green teas often have a fresh and grassy aroma, while black teas may have a malty or smoky aroma.

When selecting teas for blending, it's important to pay attention to their aroma and consider how it will contribute to the final blend. Aroma can add complexity and depth to a tea blend and can also create a sensory experience for the consumer. Some tea blends are created specifically to highlight the aroma of certain teas, such as jasmine green tea, which is prized for its delicate floral aroma.

It's also important to consider how the aroma of different teas will interact with each other in a blend. For example, a tea with a strong aroma may overpower a more delicate tea in a blend. On the other hand, two teas with complementary aromas may create a more complex and pleasing blend. When selecting teas for blending, it's essential to evaluate the aroma of each tea and how it will contribute to the overall flavor profile.

3. **Color:** The color of a tea can influence the appearance and perceived strength of the final blend. When selecting teas for blending, consider the color of each tea and how it will affect the overall appearance of the blend.

Different teas can vary in color, from light yellow or green to dark brown or red. When selecting teas for blending, it's important to consider how their colors will interact and affect the appearance of the final blend. For example, a blend of green and black teas will have a different color than a blend of only black teas. Additionally, some tea drinkers may associate a darker color with a stronger flavor, so the color of the blend can also influence the perceived strength of the tea. By considering the color of each tea and how it will interact with others in the blend, you can create a visually appealing and balanced final product.

4. **Caffeine content:** Different tea's have different levels of caffeine, which can impact the final blend's energy level. When selecting teas for blending, consider the caffeine content of each tea and how it will affect the blend's overall strength and energy level.

Caffeine content is an important factor to consider when selecting teas for blending, as it can greatly impact the energy level and overall strength of the final blend. Black teas tend to have the highest caffeine content, followed by oolong teas and green teas. Herbal teas are generally caffeine-free, while white teas contain the least amount of caffeine.

When creating a blend, consider the desired energy level of the final product. If a stronger, more energizing blend is desired, opt for teas with higher caffeine content. However, if a milder blend is desired, choose teas with lower caffeine content or incorporate herbal teas.

It's also important to keep in mind that the caffeine content of a tea can be influenced by factors such as brewing time and water temperature. Adjusting these variables can help to control the caffeine level in the final blend.

5. **Texture:** The texture of a tea can impact its mouthfeel and overall drinking experience. When selecting teas for blending, consider the texture of each tea and how it will contribute to the final blend's mouthfeel.

Texture is an often overlooked factor when selecting teas for blending, but it can greatly impact the overall drinking experience. Some teas have a smooth and silky texture, while others may be more astringent or have a rougher texture. When selecting teas for blending, consider how their texture will complement or contrast with each other. For example, a smooth and creamy tea may be balanced with a more astringent tea to create a well-rounded blend with a pleasant mouthfeel. By paying attention to the texture of each tea, you can create a blend that is not only delicious but also satisfying to drink.

By considering these factors when selecting teas for blending, you can create delicious and well-balanced tea blends that will delight your customers.

Blending Techniques and Recipes

Blending tea is a delicate art that requires expertise and creativity. Here are some common blending techniques and recipes:

1. **Simple blends: This technique involves combining two or more teas in equal parts. For example, a simple blend of black and green tea can be created by combining equal parts of each tea.**

Simple blends are a basic technique for creating tea blends by combining two or more types of tea in equal proportions. To make a simple blend of black and green tea, you can combine equal parts of both teas to create a balanced flavor profile.

Black tea is a fully oxidized tea that is known for its strong, robust flavor and caffeine content. On the other hand, green tea is an unoxidized tea that is known for its light, grassy flavor and lower caffeine content. By blending these two types of tea, you can create a unique flavor profile that balances the strength of black tea with the lightness of green tea.

To make a simple blend of black and green tea, you can start by selecting high-quality loose leaf tea of each variety. Then, mix equal parts of both teas in a container and store it in an airtight container. You can use a tea infuser or tea bag to steep the blend in hot water for a few minutes, depending on your preference for strength.

Experiment with different ratios of black and green tea to find the perfect blend for your taste buds. You can also add other ingredients such as herbs, spices, or fruits to the blend to create a more complex flavor profile. With simple blends, the possibilities are endless, so have fun and explore the world of tea!

2. **Layered blends: This technique involves layering different teas on top of each other in a teapot. For example, a layered blend of black tea and herbal tea can be created by placing the herbal tea on top of the black tea in the teapot.**

Layered blends are a technique for creating visually stunning tea blends with unique flavor profiles. This method involves layering different types of teas on top of each other in a teapot, allowing each tea to steep separately and create distinct layers of flavor.

To make a layered blend of black tea and herbal tea, you will need a teapot that has a removable infuser or strainer. First, choose high-quality loose leaf black tea and herbal tea of your choice. Place the black tea at the bottom of the teapot and fill it with hot water, allowing it to steep for the desired amount of time.

Next, carefully place the herbal tea on top of the brewed black tea. You can use a spoon or strainer to keep the layers separate. Pour hot water over the herbal tea and allow it to steep for the recommended amount of time.

As you pour the tea, you will notice the distinct layers of flavor and color. The black tea will provide a strong, robust base, while the herbal tea will add a delicate and fragrant layer on top. You can experiment with different combinations of teas and layering techniques to create your own unique blends.

It is important to note that some teas may not work well for layering. For example, teas with strong flavors, such as chai or smoked tea, may overpower the other layers and create an unbalanced flavor profile. However, with the right combination of teas and a little practice, layered blends can be a beautiful and delicious addition to any tea lover's collection.

3. **Infused blends: This technique involves infusing one type of tea with another to create a new flavor profile. For example, a green tea can be infused with dried fruit or herbs to create a fruity or herbal blend.**

Infused blends are a technique for creating tea blends by infusing one type of tea with another, as well as with herbs, fruits, or other natural ingredients. This method allows you to add new flavor profiles to your favorite teas, creating unique and delicious blends.

To make an infused blend, start by selecting high-quality loose leaf tea of your choice. Then, select the ingredients you want to infuse it with. For example, if you want to create a fruity green tea, you can infuse it with dried fruit such as mango or pineapple. Alternatively, if you want to create an herbal green tea, you can infuse it with herbs such as mint or lemongrass.

To infuse the tea, place the loose leaf tea and the ingredients in a tea infuser or tea bag. You can adjust the ratio of tea to ingredients to achieve the desired flavor profile. Place the infuser or tea bag in a teapot or mug, and pour hot water over it. Allow the tea to steep for the recommended amount of time.

As the tea steeps, the natural flavors and aromas of the infused ingredients will infuse with the tea, creating a new flavor profile. You can experiment with different combinations of tea and ingredients to create your own unique blends.
It's important to note that not all ingredients will work well for infusion. Some ingredients may overpower the flavor of the tea or create a flavor that is unpleasant. It's important to experiment with different combinations of ingredients to find the right balance.

Overall, infused blends are a fun and creative way to enjoy tea, and can provide a great way to introduce new flavors and ingredients into your tea drinking experience.

4. **Spiced blends: This technique involves adding spices, such as cinnamon or cardamom, to tea to create a warm and spicy flavor profile. For example, a black tea can be spiced with cinnamon and cloves to create a chai blend.**

Spiced blends are a technique for creating tea blends by adding spices to tea to create a warm and spicy flavor profile. This method allows you to add depth and complexity to your favorite teas, creating unique and delicious blends.

To make a spiced blend, start by selecting high-quality loose leaf tea of your choice. Then, select the spices you want to use. Popular spices for tea blends include cinnamon, cardamom, cloves, ginger, and nutmeg.

To spice the tea, place the loose leaf tea and the spices in a tea infuser or tea bag. Adjust the ratio of tea to spices to achieve the desired flavor profile. Place the infuser or tea bag in a teapot or mug, and pour hot water over it. Allow the tea to steep for the recommended amount of time.

As the tea steeps, the natural flavors and aromas of the spices will infuse with the tea, creating a warm and spicy flavor profile. You can experiment with different combinations of tea and spices to create your own unique blends.

One popular spiced blend is chai, which is made with black tea, spices, and milk. To make chai, start by spicing the tea with cinnamon, cardamom, cloves, ginger, and nutmeg. Then, add milk and sweetener to taste.

It's important to note that not all spices will work well for tea blends. Some spices may overpower the flavor of the tea or create a flavor that is unpleasant. It's important to experiment with different combinations of spices to find the right balance.

Overall, spiced blends are a delicious way to enjoy tea, and can provide a great way to introduce new flavors and spices into your tea drinking experience.

5. **Floral blends:** This technique involves adding flowers, such as rose or lavender, to tea to create a floral flavor profile. For example, a green tea can be blended with rose petals to create a delicate and floral tea blend.

Floral blends are a technique for creating tea blends by adding flowers to tea to create a delicate and floral flavor profile. This method allows you to add a subtle, yet distinctive, floral note to your favorite teas, creating unique and delicious blends.

To make a floral blend, start by selecting high-quality loose leaf tea of your choice. Then, select the flowers you want to use. Popular flowers for tea blends include rose, lavender, chamomile, and jasmine.

To blend the tea, place the loose leaf tea and the flowers in a tea infuser or tea bag. Adjust the ratio of tea to flowers to achieve the desired flavor profile. Place the infuser or tea bag in a teapot or mug, and pour hot water over it. Allow the tea to steep for the recommended amount of time.

As the tea steeps, the natural flavors and aromas of the flowers will infuse with the tea, creating a delicate and floral flavor profile. You can experiment with different combinations of tea and flowers to create your own unique blends.

One popular floral blend is rose green tea, which is made with green tea and rose petals. To make rose green tea, start by blending green tea with dried rose petals. Then, steep the tea for a few minutes in hot water. The result is a delicate and floral tea that is perfect for a relaxing afternoon.

It's important to note that not all flowers will work well for tea blends. Some flowers may overpower the flavor of the tea or create a flavor that is unpleasant. It's important to experiment with different combinations of flowers to find the right balance.

Overall, floral blends are a delicious way to enjoy tea, and can provide a great way to introduce new flavors and flowers into your tea drinking experience.

Blending tea is a highly personal and subjective process, and there are countless ways to create unique blends. Experimenting with different techniques and ingredients can lead to exciting and delicious new tea blends.

Creating signature tea blends

Creating signature tea blends is a fun and creative way to personalize your tea drinking experience. You can experiment with different combinations of tea, herbs, spices, and flowers to create unique and delicious blends that reflect your personal taste and preferences.

To create a signature tea blend, start by selecting a base tea that you enjoy, such as black tea, green tea, or herbal tea. Then, experiment with different flavor combinations by adding other ingredients to the base tea. For example, you might try blending black tea with vanilla beans, cinnamon sticks, and cardamom pods to create a warm and spicy tea blend.

When creating a signature blend, it's important to consider the balance of flavors. You don't want any one ingredient to overpower the others, but rather to create a harmonious and complex flavor profile. You can adjust the ratio of ingredients to achieve the desired flavor balance.

Another important factor to consider is the quality of the ingredients. Use high-quality loose leaf tea and fresh herbs, spices, and flowers to ensure the best possible flavor. You can also experiment with different brewing methods and steeping times to further enhance the flavor of your signature blend.

Once you've created your signature tea blend, you can share it with friends and family, or even give it as a unique and personalized gift. You can also experiment with different variations of your signature blend by adding or substituting different ingredients.

Overall, creating signature tea blends is a fun and creative way to explore new flavors and personalize your tea drinking experience. With a little experimentation and creativity, you can create unique and delicious blends that reflect your personal taste and preferences.

Tea Brewing and Tasting

Chapter 3

Tea brewing and tasting are important skills that can greatly enhance your enjoyment of tea. Proper brewing techniques and a discerning palate can help you to appreciate the subtle nuances and complexities of different tea varieties and blends.

When brewing tea, it's important to use high-quality loose leaf tea and filtered water. Bring the water to the appropriate temperature for the type of tea you are brewing. Different teas require different water temperatures to achieve the best flavor. For example, green tea is best brewed at a lower temperature of around 175°F, while black tea can be brewed at a higher temperature of around 212°F.

Measure out the appropriate amount of tea for the size of your pot or cup. Generally, a teaspoon of tea per cup is a good rule of thumb, but this can vary depending on the type of tea and your personal preference.

Allow the tea to steep for the appropriate amount of time. This can vary depending on the type of tea and your personal taste. Generally, green tea should be steeped for 1-3 minutes, while black tea can be steeped for 3-5 minutes. Herbal teas can be steeped for longer, up to 10 minutes.

When tasting tea, start by observing the appearance and aroma of the tea. Note the color of the tea and the aromas that are present. Next, take a small sip of the tea and allow it to linger in your mouth. Pay attention to the flavors and textures of the tea, noting any sweetness, bitterness, or astringency.

As you become more experienced in tasting tea, you can start to pick up on more subtle flavors and nuances. You can also experiment with different brewing methods, steeping times, and water temperatures to further enhance the flavor of the tea.

Overall, tea brewing and tasting are important skills for any tea lover. With practice and attention to detail, you can become a more discerning and appreciative tea drinker, able to fully savor the many flavors and complexities of this beloved beverage.

Basics of Tea Brewing

Brewing tea is a simple and enjoyable process that can be customized to your personal preferences. Here are some basic steps to follow when brewing tea:

1. **Choose high-quality loose leaf tea.** Loose leaf tea is generally considered to be of higher quality than tea bags, as it allows the tea leaves to expand and release their full flavor.

2. **Heat water to the appropriate temperature.** Different types of tea require different water temperatures to achieve the best flavor. As a general rule, green tea should be brewed at around 175°F, black tea at around 212°F, and white tea at around 180°F.

3. **Measure out the appropriate amount of tea.** A good rule of thumb is to use 1 teaspoon of tea per 8 ounces of water. However, you can adjust the amount of tea to suit your personal taste.

4. **Place the tea in a tea infuser or tea pot.** If using a tea infuser, place the infuser in your cup or mug. If using a tea pot, place the infuser in the pot and pour the hot water over the tea.

5. **Allow the tea to steep for the appropriate amount of time.** Different types of tea require different steeping times to achieve the best flavor. As a general rule, green tea should be steeped for 1-3 minutes, black tea for 3-5 minutes, and herbal tea for 5-10 minutes. However, you can adjust the steeping time to suit your personal taste.

6. **Remove the tea infuser or strain the tea**. Once the tea has steeped for the appropriate amount of time, remove the tea infuser or strain the tea to remove the tea leaves.

7. **Enjoy your tea!** Add any sweeteners or milk as desired, and savor the delicious flavor and aroma of your freshly brewed tea.

By following these basic steps, you can brew a delicious cup of tea that is customized to your personal taste. Experiment with different types of tea, water temperatures, and steeping times to find the perfect brewing method for you.

Different brewing methods and their effects on tea flavor

There are several different brewing methods that can be used to prepare tea, and each method can affect the flavor and aroma of the tea in different ways. Here are some common brewing methods and their effects on tea flavor:

1. **Western-style brewing: This is the most common brewing method used in the West. It involves steeping tea leaves in a teapot or infuser for 3-5 minutes, then pouring the tea into a cup. This method tends to produce a balanced flavor profile, with a moderate level of astringency.**

Western-style brewing is a popular method for preparing tea in the West. It is simple and straightforward, making it an easy way for beginners to start exploring the world of tea.

The basic steps of Western-style brewing involve placing tea leaves in a teapot or infuser, adding hot water, and allowing the tea to steep for 3-5 minutes. After steeping, the tea is poured into a cup and enjoyed.

This brewing method tends to produce a balanced flavor profile, with a moderate level of astringency. The flavors and aromas of the tea are extracted during steeping, resulting in a full-bodied and flavorful cup of tea. However, this method may not be suitable for all types of tea, as some delicate or high-quality teas may require more precise brewing methods to fully express their unique flavors and characteristics.

Overall, Western-style brewing is a great starting point for those new to tea and provides a convenient and simple way to enjoy a cup of tea. With a little experimentation and practice, anyone can learn to brew the perfect cup of tea using this method.

2. **Gongfu brewing:** This is a traditional Chinese brewing method that involves steeping tea leaves in a small clay teapot multiple times for short durations, usually less than a minute. This method can enhance the complexity and subtlety of the tea's flavor, as well as increase its aroma and intensity.

Gongfu brewing is a traditional Chinese brewing method that has been practiced for centuries. It involves steeping tea leaves in a small clay teapot multiple times for short durations, usually less than a minute. This method is highly valued for its ability to enhance the complexity and subtlety of the tea's flavor, as well as increase its aroma and intensity.

The Gongfu brewing process involves several steps, including:

1. **Preparing the teapot and teaware:** The teapot and teaware should be clean and heated before use to ensure that the tea brews evenly and at the right temperature.

2. **Measuring the tea leaves:** The amount of tea leaves used depends on the size of the teapot and personal preference. Generally, 5-7 grams of tea leaves are used for a small 100ml teapot.

3. **Pre-rinsing the tea leaves:** Rinse the tea leaves with hot water for a few seconds to remove any dust or impurities and to "wake up" the tea.

4. **First infusion:** Add hot water to the teapot and let the tea steep for a short duration, usually around 5-10 seconds.

5. **Pouring and serving:** After the first infusion, pour the tea into a small pitcher or fairness cup and then serve into small teacups. The tea should be poured in a circular motion to ensure an even distribution of flavor.

6. **Subsequent infusions**: The tea leaves can be re-infused multiple times, with each infusion lasting a little longer than the previous one. The brewing time can be adjusted based on personal preference and the characteristics of the tea being brewed.

The Gongfu brewing method requires patience, precision, and attention to detail. It is ideal for high-quality teas such as oolongs, pu-erhs, and some green teas that have complex flavor profiles and can be steeped multiple times. The resulting tea is often highly fragrant, full-bodied, and deeply satisfying, making it a favorite of tea connoisseurs around the world.

3. **Cold brewing: This method involves steeping tea leaves in cold water for several hours. Cold brewing can produce a smoother and less bitter flavor profile, with less astringency and more sweetness.**

Cold brewing is a method of brewing tea that involves steeping tea leaves in cold water for several hours. This method is particularly popular during the summer months, as it produces a refreshing and low-acidic tea that can be served chilled. Here are the steps to cold brew tea:

1. Choose a tea that is suitable for cold brewing. Generally, it is recommended to use high-quality loose-leaf tea, as it tends to produce a better flavor. Popular teas for cold brewing include green tea, black tea, oolong tea, and herbal teas.

2. Measure out the tea leaves. A good rule of thumb is to use about 1 tablespoon of tea leaves for every 8-12 ounces of water.

3. Place the tea leaves in a pitcher or container.

4. Add cold water to the pitcher or container. It is recommended to use filtered water to ensure that the tea does not pick up any off-flavors from the tap water.

5. Stir the tea leaves and water together to ensure that the leaves are fully submerged.

6. Cover the pitcher or container and place it in the refrigerator.

7. Allow the tea to steep for several hours, usually 6-12 hours, depending on the type of tea and personal taste preference.

8. Once the tea has steeped to your desired strength, strain the tea leaves out of the pitcher or container.

9. Serve the cold-brewed tea over ice, with optional additions such as fresh fruit or herbs.

Overall, cold brewing is a simple and low-maintenance method of brewing tea that can produce a refreshing and unique flavor profile. It is important to note that cold brewing may require a longer steeping time than traditional hot brewing methods, so patience is key.

4. **Grandpa-style brewing: This is a simple brewing method used in China that involves placing tea leaves directly in a cup or mug, then adding hot water and drinking directly from the cup. This method can produce a milder flavor profile, with less bitterness and astringency.**

Grandpa-style brewing is a simple and convenient method of brewing tea. Here are the steps:

1. Select your tea leaves: Choose high-quality loose-leaf tea for the best results.

2. Add tea leaves to your cup: Add 1-2 teaspoons of tea leaves directly to your cup or mug.

3. Add hot water: Pour hot water over the tea leaves, filling the cup about halfway.

4. Let the tea steep: Allow the tea to steep for 3-5 minutes, or until it reaches your desired strength.

5. Top off with hot water: Add more hot water to fill the cup to the desired level.

6. Enjoy: Sip the tea directly from the cup, or use a strainer to remove the tea leaves if desired.

This method is called Grandpa-style because it is often used by older Chinese people who prefer a milder and less intense flavor profile. It is a quick and easy way to enjoy a cup of tea without the need for a teapot or strainer.

5. **Whisked brewing: This method is used to prepare powdered green tea, such as matcha. It involves whisking the powdered tea in hot water to create a frothy and creamy beverage. This method can produce a smooth and velvety texture, as well as a rich and complex flavor profile.**

Whisked brewing is a traditional Japanese method used to prepare powdered green tea, such as matcha. This method is known for producing a smooth and velvety texture, as well as a rich and complex flavor profile. Here are the steps to prepare whisked tea:

1. **Heat water:** Heat water to a temperature of about 175-180°F (80-82°C). It's important not to use boiling water, as this can damage the delicate flavor of the tea.

2. **Sift tea:** Sift about 1-2 teaspoons of powdered tea into a bowl. This helps to remove any clumps and ensure a smooth texture.

3. **Add water**: Pour a small amount of hot water (about 1-2 ounces) into the bowl, and use a bamboo whisk to mix the tea and water together into a paste.

4. **Add remaining water:** Pour the rest of the hot water into the bowl, and use the whisk to mix the tea until it becomes frothy and creamy.

5. **Serve:** Pour the whisked tea into a cup and enjoy immediately. Whisked tea should be consumed right away to ensure the best flavor and texture.

Overall, whisked brewing is a unique and enjoyable way to prepare powdered green tea, and is perfect for those who enjoy a rich and complex flavor profile.

Overall, different brewing methods can have a significant impact on the flavor and aroma of the tea. Experiment with different brewing methods to discover the ones that best suit your personal taste preferences.

Tea Tasting Techniques and Sensory Evaluation

Tea tasting is a sensory experience that involves evaluating the appearance, aroma, and taste of different types of tea. Here are some common tea tasting techniques and sensory evaluation methods:

1. **Appearance: The appearance of the tea can provide important clues about its quality and flavor. Look for factors such as the color of the brewed tea, the size and shape of the tea leaves, and the clarity of the liquid.**

   1. **Examine the color of the brewed tea:** Observe the color of the brewed tea to identify its quality. High-quality teas typically have a vibrant and consistent color, while lower quality teas may have a dull or inconsistent color.

   2. **Check the size and shape of the tea leaves:** High-quality tea leaves are often whole or large pieces, while lower quality teas may contain smaller, broken pieces or tea dust.

   3. **Observe the clarity of the liquid:** The liquid of high-quality teas tends to be clear and bright, while lower quality teas may have a cloudy or murky appearance.

   4. **Look for any foreign objects:** Check the tea leaves for any foreign objects or other plant material that may have been mixed in during processing.

   5. **Evaluate the overall appearance:** After examining each of these factors, evaluate the overall appearance of the tea to assess its quality and potential flavor profile.

2. **Aroma: The aroma of the tea can be evaluated by smelling the brewed tea. Inhale deeply and take note of the different aromas present, such as floral, earthy, or fruity notes.**

1. Take a clean and dry tea cup or bowl and pour the brewed tea into it.

2. Hold the cup or bowl close to your nose and inhale deeply, taking note of the different aromas present.

3. Consider the intensity and complexity of the aroma. Does it have a strong or subtle scent? Can you detect multiple notes or just one dominant aroma?

4. Try to identify the specific scents present, such as floral, fruity, herbal, or spicy notes.

5. Consider how the aroma may change over time as the tea cools or steeps for longer periods.

6. Remember that the aroma can provide important clues about the quality and flavor of the tea. A strong and complex aroma may indicate a high-quality tea with a rich and nuanced flavor.

3. **Taste: The taste of the tea is perhaps the most important aspect of tea tasting. Take a small sip and let the tea sit on your tongue for a few seconds before swallowing. Note the different flavor profiles present, such as sweetness, bitterness, and astringency.**

Here are the steps to evaluate the taste of tea:

1. Take a small sip of the brewed tea and let it sit on your tongue for a few seconds.

2. Swirl the tea around in your mouth, coating your tongue and tasting buds.

3. Note the different flavors that you can detect, such as sweetness, bitterness, and astringency.

4. Pay attention to the aftertaste or finish of the tea. Does it linger pleasantly or leave an unpleasant taste in your mouth?

5. Take another sip and see if the taste changes or evolves as the tea cools or as you drink more of it.

It is also helpful to compare the taste of different teas side by side to better understand the differences in flavor profiles.

4. **Mouthfeel: The mouthfeel of the tea refers to its texture and consistency in the mouth. Note the thickness, smoothness, and dryness of the tea.**

Sure, here are the steps for evaluating the mouthfeel of tea:

1. Take a small sip of the tea and let it coat your mouth.

2. Pay attention to the texture of the tea. Is it thin or thick in consistency? Does it feel smooth or rough on your tongue?

3. Note any sensations in your mouth, such as dryness or astringency. Is the tea drying out your mouth or leaving a lingering aftertaste?

4. Consider the overall balance of the mouthfeel. Does it complement the tea's flavor or overpower it?

5. **Aftertaste: The aftertaste of the tea refers to the flavors that linger in the mouth after swallowing. Note the length and intensity of the aftertaste, as well as any changes in flavor that occur over time.**

The aftertaste of the tea is an important aspect of tea tasting that can provide insight into the tea's overall quality and complexity. After swallowing the tea, note the lingering flavors that remain in the mouth. A high-quality tea will often have a long and pleasant aftertaste with nuanced flavor notes that continue to evolve. On the other hand, a low-quality tea may have a short and unpleasant aftertaste, with strong bitterness or astringency. The aftertaste can also provide information about the tea's origin and processing, such as notes of terroir or hints of smoke or woodiness. Overall, the aftertaste is an essential aspect of tea tasting that should be evaluated alongside appearance, aroma, taste, and mouthfeel.

To evaluate teas more systematically, professionals often use a standardized testing process called "cupping." This process involves brewing a small amount of tea in a standardized vessel, then evaluating the appearance, aroma, and taste of the tea using a standardized scoring system. Cupping is commonly used in the tea industry to evaluate the quality of different teas and to develop new blends.

By using these techniques and methods, you can improve your tea tasting skills and gain a deeper appreciation for the complex flavors and aromas of different types of tea.

How to evaluate tea quality ?

Evaluating tea quality involves assessing several key factors that contribute to the overall flavor and aroma of the tea. Here are some key factors to consider when evaluating tea quality:

1. **Appearance:** Look for tea leaves that are whole, uniform in size and color, and free from stems, twigs, or other foreign matter. The appearance of the brewed tea should also be clear and bright, with a consistent color and no sediment.

2. **Aroma:** The aroma of the tea should be fresh, clean, and free from any off-notes or musty odors. The aroma should be indicative of the tea's origin and processing, such as floral notes in a high-quality green tea or earthy notes in a pu-erh tea.

3. **Flavor:** The flavor of the tea should be complex, balanced, and free from any bitterness, astringency, or off-flavors. The flavor should be consistent with the tea's origin and processing, such as nutty flavors in a high-quality oolong tea or fruity notes in a Darjeeling tea.

4. **Mouthfeel:** The mouthfeel of the tea should be smooth, silky, and full-bodied, with no grittiness or harshness. The texture should complement the flavor of the tea and enhance its overall drinking experience.

5. **Aftertaste:** The aftertaste of the tea should be long-lasting and pleasant, with no off-notes or lingering bitterness. The aftertaste should enhance the overall drinking experience and leave a positive impression on the palate.

In addition to these factors, the quality of the water used to brew the tea, the brewing time and temperature, and the vessel used to brew and serve the tea can all have an impact on the overall quality and flavor of the tea. By paying attention to these factors and using them to guide your tea selection and preparation, you can develop a deeper appreciation for the complex and nuanced flavors of high-quality teas.

Tea Marketing and Sales
Chapter 4

Tea marketing and sales involve promoting and selling different types of teas to consumers. Here are some key strategies and techniques that can be used to effectively market and sell tea:

1. **Product differentiation:** Differentiating your tea products from those of your competitors is key to attracting and retaining customers. This can be achieved through offering unique blends, packaging, or origin stories that set your teas apart from others in the market.

2. **Branding:** Developing a strong brand identity that resonates with your target audience can help to build brand loyalty and differentiate your teas from others in the market. This can involve creating a unique brand name, logo, and messaging that reflects the values and qualities of your teas.

3. **Sampling:** Offering samples of your teas to potential customers is a highly effective marketing technique, as it allows customers to try your teas before making a purchase. This can be done through in-store sampling or by offering free samples with online orders.

4. **Online sales and marketing**: E-commerce platforms and social media channels can be highly effective tools for marketing and selling teas. By creating an engaging online presence and leveraging social media to promote your teas and connect with customers, you can reach a wider audience and drive sales.

5. **Special promotions and events**: Offering special promotions, discounts, and events can help to generate excitement around your teas and incentivize customers to make a purchase. This can include offering limited-

edition blends, hosting tea tastings or pairing events, or offering seasonal discounts and promotions.

6. **Collaborations and partnerships:** Collaborating with other businesses or influencers in the food and beverage industry can help to increase visibility and generate interest in your teas. This can involve partnering with restaurants or cafes to offer your teas on their menus, or collaborating with food bloggers or social media influencers to promote your teas to their followers.

By using these strategies and techniques to effectively market and sell your teas, you can build a loyal customer base and increase your revenue over time.

Developing a brand identity for your tea business

Developing a strong brand identity is essential for creating a recognizable and successful tea business. Here are some key steps to take when developing your brand identity:

1. **Define your target audience:** Knowing your target audience is key to developing a brand identity that resonates with your customers. Consider factors such as age, gender, income, lifestyle, and values to help define your target audience.

2. **Create a unique name and logo**: Your brand name and logo should be unique and memorable, reflecting the values and qualities of your tea business. Consider using a name and logo that conveys your tea's origin story, unique flavor profile, or other distinguishing features.

3. **Develop your brand messaging:** Your brand messaging should communicate the unique value proposition of your tea business, such as the quality, taste, or sustainability of your teas. Use messaging that resonates with your target audience and sets your brand apart from competitors.

4. **Choose your brand colors and design:** The color palette and overall design of your branding materials, such as packaging and marketing materials, should be consistent with your brand messaging and appeal to your target audience.

5. **Establish your brand voice**: Your brand voice should be consistent across all communication channels, such as social media, advertising, and customer service. Consider the tone and language that best resonates with your target audience.

6. **Build your online presence:** Establishing a strong online presence is essential for promoting your brand and engaging with customers. Create a website and social media channels that showcase your brand identity and regularly share content that resonates with your target audience.

Creating a marketing plan for your tea products

Creating a marketing plan is an important step in promoting and selling your tea products. Here are some key steps to consider when creating a marketing plan for your tea business:

1. **Define your target audience:** Start by defining your target audience based on factors such as age, gender, income, lifestyle, and values. Understanding your target audience will help you tailor your marketing messages to resonate with them.

2. **Identify your unique selling proposition (USP):** What sets your tea products apart from competitors? Your USP could be your tea's unique flavor profile, quality, or sustainability practices. Make sure to highlight your USP in all of your marketing materials.

3. **Determine your marketing channels:** Consider the most effective marketing channels for reaching your target audience, such as social media, email marketing, influencer marketing, events, and collaborations with other businesses.

4. **Develop your marketing messages:** Your marketing messages should be tailored to your target audience and highlight your USP. Use language and messaging that resonates with your target audience and sets your brand apart from competitors.

5. **Create a content calendar:** Plan out your marketing activities on a calendar, including social media posts, email newsletters, and events. This will help ensure that your marketing efforts are consistent and coordinated.

6. **Set marketing goals and metrics**: Determine specific marketing goals, such as increasing website traffic or sales, and track your progress using metrics such as website analytics and sales data.

7. **Measure and adjust your marketing plan:** Regularly review your marketing efforts to determine what's working and what's not. Adjust your marketing plan as needed to optimize your results.

By following these steps, you can create a comprehensive marketing plan that helps you effectively promote and sell your tea products. Remember to stay consistent, monitor your progress, and adjust your plan as needed to achieve your marketing goals.

Online and Offline Sales Strategies

Here are some online and offline sales strategies you can consider for your tea business:

Online sales strategies

- **E-commerce website:** Create an e-commerce website where customers can browse and purchase your tea products online. Make sure the website is user-friendly, visually appealing, and has detailed product descriptions and high-quality images.

- **Social media:** Use social media platforms such as Instagram, Facebook, and Twitter to promote your tea products, engage with your followers, and drive traffic to your website. Consider using social media ads to target specific audiences.

- **Email marketing:** Build an email list of customers and send them newsletters and promotional emails to keep them engaged and informed about your tea products.

- **Influencer marketing:** Collaborate with social media influencers who have a large following in your target audience to promote your tea products.

- **Online marketplaces:** Sell your tea products on online marketplaces such as Amazon, Etsy, and eBay to reach a wider audience.

Offline Sales Strategies

- **Pop-up shops**: Set up temporary pop-up shops in high-traffic areas such as farmers markets, festivals, and shopping malls to showcase your tea products and sell directly to customers.

- **Retail stores:** Partner with local retail stores that align with your brand values and target audience to sell your tea products.

- **Tastings and events:** Host tastings and events to promote your tea products and engage with potential customers. Partner with other businesses or organizations to host joint events.

- **Wholesale:** Sell your tea products in bulk to restaurants, cafes, and other businesses that serve tea to their customers.

By utilizing a combination of online and offline sales strategies, you can reach a wider audience and increase sales for your tea business. Make sure to track your sales and marketing efforts to determine what's working and adjust your strategies as needed to optimize your results.

Setting Prices and Managing Inventory

Setting the right prices and managing inventory are critical components of running a successful tea business. Here are some tips to consider:

1. **Setting prices**

- **Determine your costs:** Calculate the costs of ingredients, packaging, labor, and overhead expenses to determine the total cost of producing each unit of tea.
- **Research the market:** Look at the prices of similar tea products in the market to determine a competitive price range.

- **Consider your target audience:** Determine what price range your target audience is willing to pay for your tea products.

- **Set your profit margins:** Decide on your desired profit margin for each unit of tea and adjust your pricing accordingly.

2. **Managing inventory**

- **Keep track of your inventory levels**: Use inventory management software to track your stock levels and sales to ensure that you have enough inventory to meet customer demand.

- **Use forecasting:** Use historical sales data and industry trends to forecast future demand and plan your inventory levels accordingly.

- **Order in advance:** Place orders with your suppliers in advance to ensure that you have enough inventory to meet demand and avoid stockouts.

- **Optimize your inventory:** Avoid overstocking or understocking by optimizing your inventory levels based on demand and sales data.

By setting the right prices and managing inventory effectively, you can ensure that your tea business is profitable and can meet customer demand.

Managing a Tea Business
Chapter 5

Managing a tea business requires a combination of business, marketing, and tea-related skills. Here are some key areas to focus on when managing a tea business:

1. **Business operations**

- **Create a business plan**: Develop a business plan that outlines your goals, target audience, marketing strategy, financial projections, and operations.

- **Obtain necessary permits and licenses**: Research and obtain any necessary permits and licenses required to operate your tea business.

- **Set up a workspace:** Set up a workspace that includes all the necessary equipment and supplies for tea production, such as tea brewing equipment, packaging materials, and storage.

- **Develop a supply chain:** Establish relationships with tea suppliers and other vendors to ensure that you have access to high-quality tea ingredients and supplies.

2. **Marketing and sales**

- **Develop a brand identity:** Create a brand identity that reflects your company values, mission, and target audience.

- **Develop a marketing plan:** Develop a marketing plan that includes online and offline sales strategies, promotional tactics, and customer outreach.

- **Build an online presence:** Develop a strong online presence through social media, email marketing, and e-commerce to reach a wider audience.

- **Attend events and tastings:** Attend industry events and tastings to connect with other tea professionals and potential customers.

3. **Tea knowledge and production**

- **Develop tea knowledge:** Develop a strong knowledge of tea production, tea varieties, brewing methods, and flavor profiles to create high-quality tea products.

- **Develop unique tea blends:** Experiment with different tea blends and flavor combinations to develop unique and marketable tea products.

- **Monitor quality:** Monitor tea quality through regular taste tests and quality control measures to ensure consistent flavor and quality in every batch.

4. **Financial management**

- **Set financial goals:** Set financial goals and develop a financial plan that includes revenue targets, cost projections, and profit margins.

- **Monitor financial performance:** Track your financial performance regularly to ensure that you are meeting your goals and adjust your strategies as needed.

- **Manage expenses:** Manage your expenses carefully by optimizing your inventory, minimizing waste, and controlling costs.

By focusing on these key areas, you can successfully manage a tea business and build a loyal customer base that appreciates high-quality tea products.

Legal and regulatory considerations for tea businesses

There are several legal and regulatory considerations that tea businesses need to be aware of, including:

1. **Permits and Licenses:** Tea businesses may need to obtain specific permits and licenses to operate, depending on their location and the type of tea business they are running. These may include food service permits, business licenses, and state-specific permits for tea production.

2. **Food Safety Regulations:** Tea businesses must comply with local, state, and federal food safety regulations to ensure that their products are safe for consumption. This includes following good manufacturing practices, adhering to labeling requirements, and maintaining appropriate records.

3. **Intellectual Property Protection:** Tea businesses may need to protect their intellectual property, such as their brand name, logos, and packaging designs, through trademarks, patents, or copyrights.

4. **Import and Export Regulations:** Tea businesses that import or export tea products must comply with international trade regulations, including customs requirements, tariffs, and product safety standards.

5. **Labor Laws:** Tea businesses must comply with labor laws, including minimum wage and overtime requirements, workplace safety regulations, and anti-discrimination laws.

It is important for tea businesses to stay up to date with these legal and regulatory considerations to ensure compliance and avoid potential legal issues. It may be helpful to consult with legal professionals or industry associations for guidance on specific regulations and requirements.

Managing Finances and Cash Flow

Managing finances and cash flow is an essential aspect of running a successful tea business. Here are some key considerations for managing finances and cash flow:

1. **Develop a budget:** Creating a budget is a critical first step in managing finances. A budget helps tea businesses to identify their expenses and revenue sources and allocate funds accordingly. It is essential to review and update the budget regularly to ensure that it remains relevant and accurate.

2. **Keep accurate financial records:** Tea businesses should keep accurate financial records, including receipts, invoices, and bank statements. This will help to track income and expenses, identify potential issues early, and make informed decisions about the business's financial management.

3. **Monitor cash flow:** Tea businesses should closely monitor their cash flow to ensure that they have enough funds to cover expenses and invest in the business's growth. This involves tracking incoming and outgoing cash, projecting future cash flow, and identifying potential cash flow issues.

4. **Manage inventory:** Effective inventory management is crucial for managing cash flow. Tea businesses should maintain an appropriate level of inventory to meet customer demand while avoiding excess inventory that ties up cash.

5. **Consider financing options:** Tea businesses may need to consider financing options, such as loans or lines of credit, to manage cash flow or invest in the business's growth. It is important to research and compare financing options to find the best fit for the business's needs and budget.

Managing finances and cash flow can be complex, and tea businesses may benefit from seeking the guidance of financial professionals, such as accountants or financial advisors.

Hiring and Training Staff

Hiring and training staff is an important aspect of managing a successful tea business. Here are some key considerations for hiring and training staff:

1. **Determine staffing needs:** Tea businesses should determine their staffing needs based on the size of the business, the level of customer demand, and the scope of operations. This will help to ensure that the business has the right number of staff to meet customer needs and manage operations effectively.

2. **Develop job descriptions:** Tea businesses should develop clear job descriptions for each position, outlining the roles and responsibilities of each staff member. This will help to ensure that staff understand their duties and are able to perform their job effectively.

3. **Recruit and hire qualified staff:** Tea businesses should recruit and hire staff who are qualified and have the necessary skills and experience to perform their job effectively. This may involve advertising job openings, reviewing resumes and applications, and conducting interviews.

4. **Provide training and development:** Tea businesses should provide staff with training and development opportunities to help them perform their job effectively and grow professionally. This may include on-the-job training, workshops, and continuing education opportunities.

5. **Establish clear policies and procedures:** Tea businesses should establish clear policies and procedures for staff to follow, including policies related to customer service, safety, and operations. This will help to ensure that staff understand what is expected of them and can perform their job effectively.

Hiring and training staff can be time-consuming and costly, but it is essential for the success of the business. Tea businesses may benefit from seeking the guidance of human resources professionals or industry associations for guidance on best practices for hiring and training staff.

Developing a sustainable and socially responsible tea business

Developing a sustainable and socially responsible tea business is becoming increasingly important as consumers become more conscious of the environmental and social impacts of their purchasing decisions. Here are some key considerations for developing a sustainable and socially responsible tea business:

1. **Sustainable sourcing:** Tea businesses should consider sourcing their tea from sustainable and environmentally responsible suppliers. This may involve selecting suppliers who use sustainable farming practices, minimize waste, and reduce their carbon footprint.

2. **Social responsibility:** Tea businesses should consider the social impacts of their operations, including labor practices and community engagement. This may involve ensuring fair labor practices throughout the supply chain and supporting local communities through philanthropic initiatives or partnerships.

3. **Environmental impact:** Tea businesses should consider the environmental impacts of their operations, including energy use, waste management, and packaging. This may involve reducing energy use, minimizing waste, and using eco-friendly packaging.

4. **Education and outreach:** Tea businesses can educate their customers about the importance of sustainability and social responsibility through marketing and outreach efforts. This may involve providing information about the company's sustainable and socially responsible practices, and encouraging customers to make environmentally and socially conscious purchasing decisions.

5. **Continuous improvement:** Tea businesses should continuously evaluate and improve their sustainability and social responsibility practices to ensure that they are making a positive impact. This may involve setting goals and metrics for sustainability and social responsibility, and regularly reviewing and reporting on progress.

Developing a sustainable and socially responsible tea business requires a commitment to ongoing improvement and a willingness to invest in sustainable and socially responsible practices. However, these efforts can have a positive impact on the environment, local communities, and the long-term success of the business.

Conclusion

In conclusion, managing a tea business requires a range of skills and knowledge, including expertise in tea cultivation, production, blending, brewing, marketing, and sales. Additionally, it is increasingly important for tea businesses to adopt sustainable and socially responsible practices that address environmental and social impacts. By investing in sustainable sourcing, social responsibility, environmental impact reduction, education and outreach, and continuous improvement, tea businesses can not only improve their own operations but also contribute to positive change in the world. With a commitment to quality, innovation, and sustainability, tea businesses can build a loyal customer base and achieve long-term success.

All the best for your successful future.

Milton Keynes UK
Ingram Content Group UK Ltd.
UKHW051030221123
433051UK00018B/706

9 798215 300886